A Day in the Life of a...

Firefighter

Carol Watson

Watts Books
London ● New York ● Sydney

This is Sarah. She is a firefighter.
Sarah works at a fire station
in West London.

Sarah's team of firefighters is called the White Watch. They start work by going on parade.

The watch commander inspects
the firefighters to make sure that
they all have the correct
uniform and equipment.

Then Sarah puts her fire-gear into the engine ready to use.

"Time to check the equipment," she tells James.

The equipment is stored on either side of the fire engine. It includes hoses, ropes, brushes, extinguishers and lights.

The ladder lies on top of the engine, and inside there is a huge tank which holds over 1000 litres of water.

"We'll do a drill
this morning," says
the commander.
The White Watch
practise using
the equipment.

There is a tall tower
in the yard so the
firefighters can
practise climbing into
high buildings, too.

Firefighters need to
know how to tie all sorts
of knots so they can
haul up the things they need.

They are also trained to cut
people out of cars
so that they can help anyone
trapped in road accidents.

During the tea break, the fire alarm rings. "I'll get the details," says Mick.

He gets the information from the teleprinter.

White Watch
leave their tea
and quickly go
into action.
They slide down
the pole and rush
to the fire engine.

13

"There's a fire in Church Road," Mick tells the firefighters. They put on their gear and the engine sets out.

At the scene of the fire the firefighters unroll the hoses. Grant attaches one to the fire hydrant in the street to get extra water.

Two of the firefighters put on their breathing masks. The entry control officer writes down who is going into the building.

Sarah and Grant enter the
smoky building carrying a
hose to put out the fire.
It is very dark inside.

The fire is out.
Ian rolls up one
of the hoses.

Then he puts
it back in the
machine and
the firefighters
return to the
fire station.

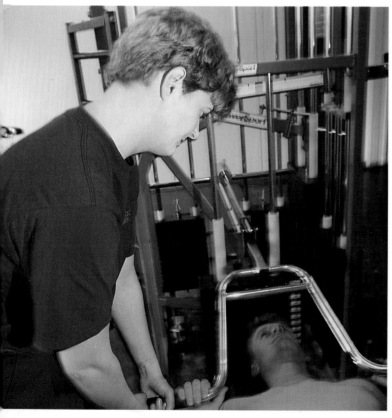

Back at the fire station the White Watch end their shift exercising in the gym.

Now Sarah is off duty, she can go home.

Make a Fire Action Plan

You will need:

a large sheet of white paper

a black felt tip pen

a red felt tip pen

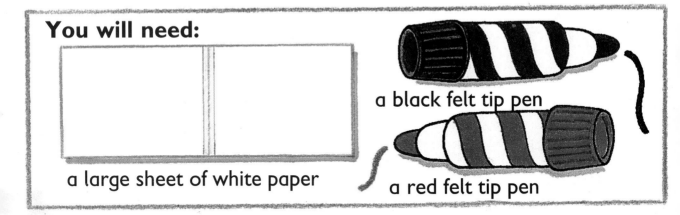

FIRE ACTION PLAN

1. Close the door of the room where the fire is burning.

2. Shout loudly to warn everyone.

3. Get everyone out of the house.
   GET OUT AND STAY OUT!

4. Warn the neighbours.

5. If you are trapped in your room, put clothes
   or bedding beneath the door to block the smoke.

6. **DIAL 999** and ask for the Fire Brigade.
   Tell the operator your full address and the
   NEAREST MAIN ROAD.

What would you do in a fire?
Which is the nearest way out of your house?
Make a Fire Action Plan and stick it on your bedroom door.
Draw a plan of your house. Mark the danger zones in red,
and your escape route out of the house.

> **Danger zones: gas or electric fires, heaters, cookers, boiler and electric blankets. Anyone who smokes.**

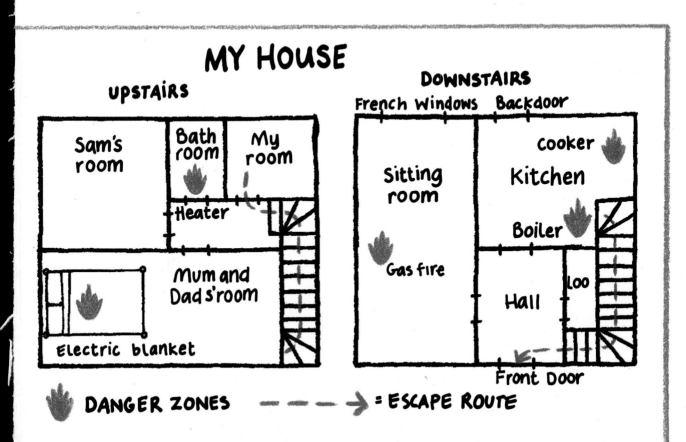

MY HOUSE

UPSTAIRS

Sam's room

Bath room

My room

Heater

Mum and Dad's room

Electric blanket

DOWNSTAIRS

French Windows   Backdoor

cooker

Kitchen

Sitting room

Boiler

Gas fire

Hall

Loo

Front Door

DANGER ZONES   ----→ = ESCAPE ROUTE

How you can help the firefighters

1. Don't go near a fire or cooker.

2. Never play with matches or a lighter.

3. Don't leave your toys near a fire or a heater.

4. Don't leave a newspaper or comic on top of a heater.

5. Learn what to do in a fire. Make a fire action plan.

6. Never go into a burning building to find a pet or a toy.

Facts about firefighters

It takes four years to become a fully qualified firefighter. This begins with 20 weeks at a training centre. After that the firefighter is posted to a fire station.

As well as putting out fires, firefighters carry out many other services. They check the area water supply and inspect the fire escapes and firefighting equipment of schools, offices and hotels.

Firefighters attend road traffic accidents and rescue people and pets that are trapped. They also rescue people from floods and pump the water out of their homes.

The fire station in this book is open day and night. There are two fire engines and at least eight firefighters on duty on each watch all the time, even on Christmas Day.

Index

©1995 Watts Books

Watts Books
96 Leonard Street
London EC2A 4RH

Franklin Watts Australia
14 Mars Road
Lane Cove
NSW 2066

UK ISBN: 0 7496 1995 3
Dewey Decimal
Classification Number 363.3
10 9 8 7 6 5 4 3 2 1
A CIP catalogue record for
this book is available from
the British Library.

Printed in Malaysia

Editor: Sarah Ridley
Designer: Nina Kingsbury
Photographer: Chris Honeywell
Illustration pgs 20-21: Andrew
   Crowson

With thanks to Station Commander
Michael Quy, Mairead Moore and the
members of the White Watch,
Chiswick Fire Station.